Contents

Meet Anna the nurse

This is
Nurse Anna.

4

Nurse Anna works at this hospital.

Before work

Anna gets Daniel out of bed.

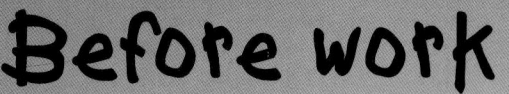

She then eats breakfast
with her family.

The day starts

Anna changes into her uniform at work.

Doctor Charles

9

The first patient

Mary-Ann tells Anna
she hurt her arm.
She had a nightmare
and fell out of bed.

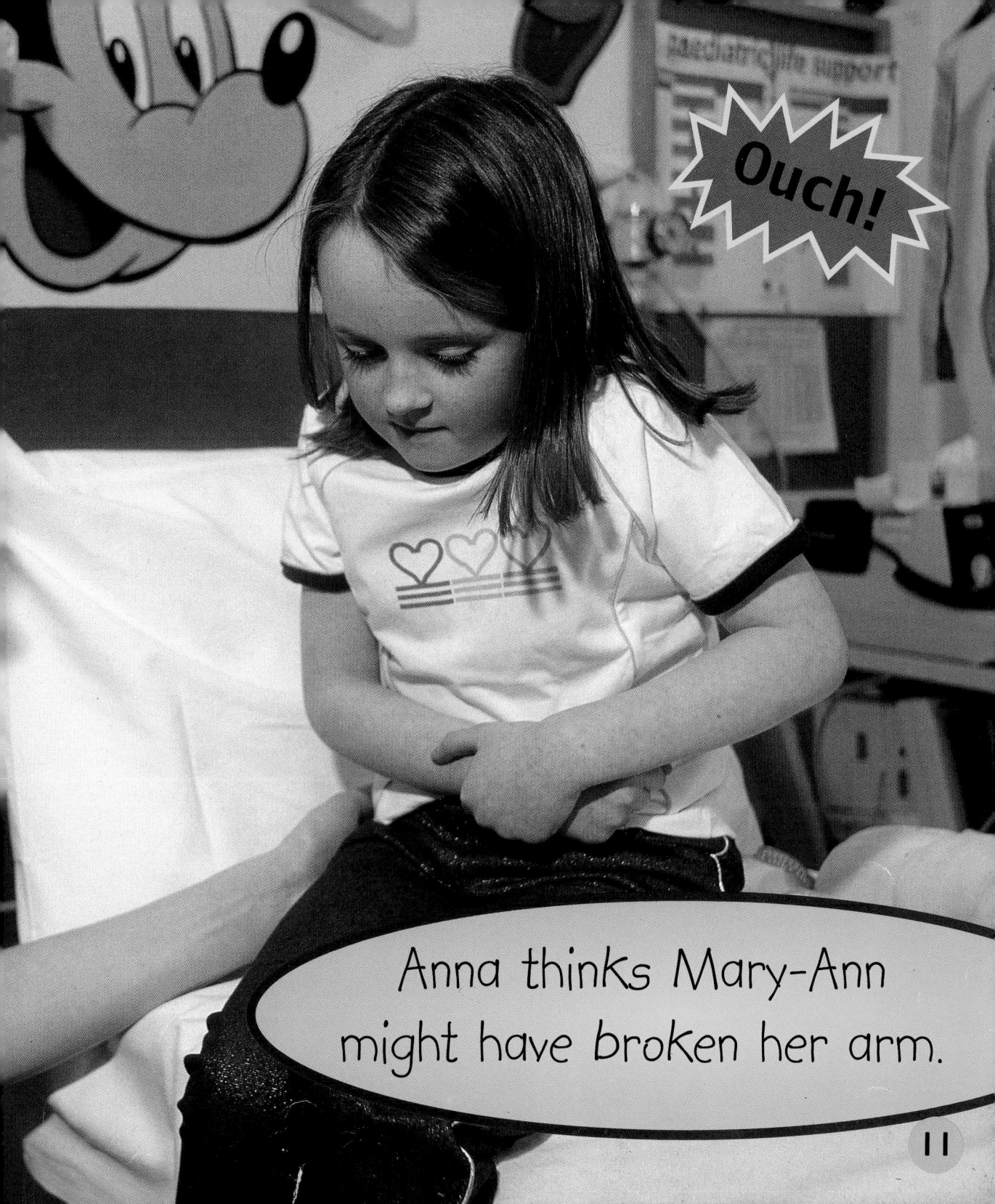

An X-ray

Anna shows Mary-Ann the X-ray of her arm. It's not broken.

Anna puts Mary-Ann's arm
into a sling.

13

More patients

Anna takes the temperature of a boy who is not feeling well.

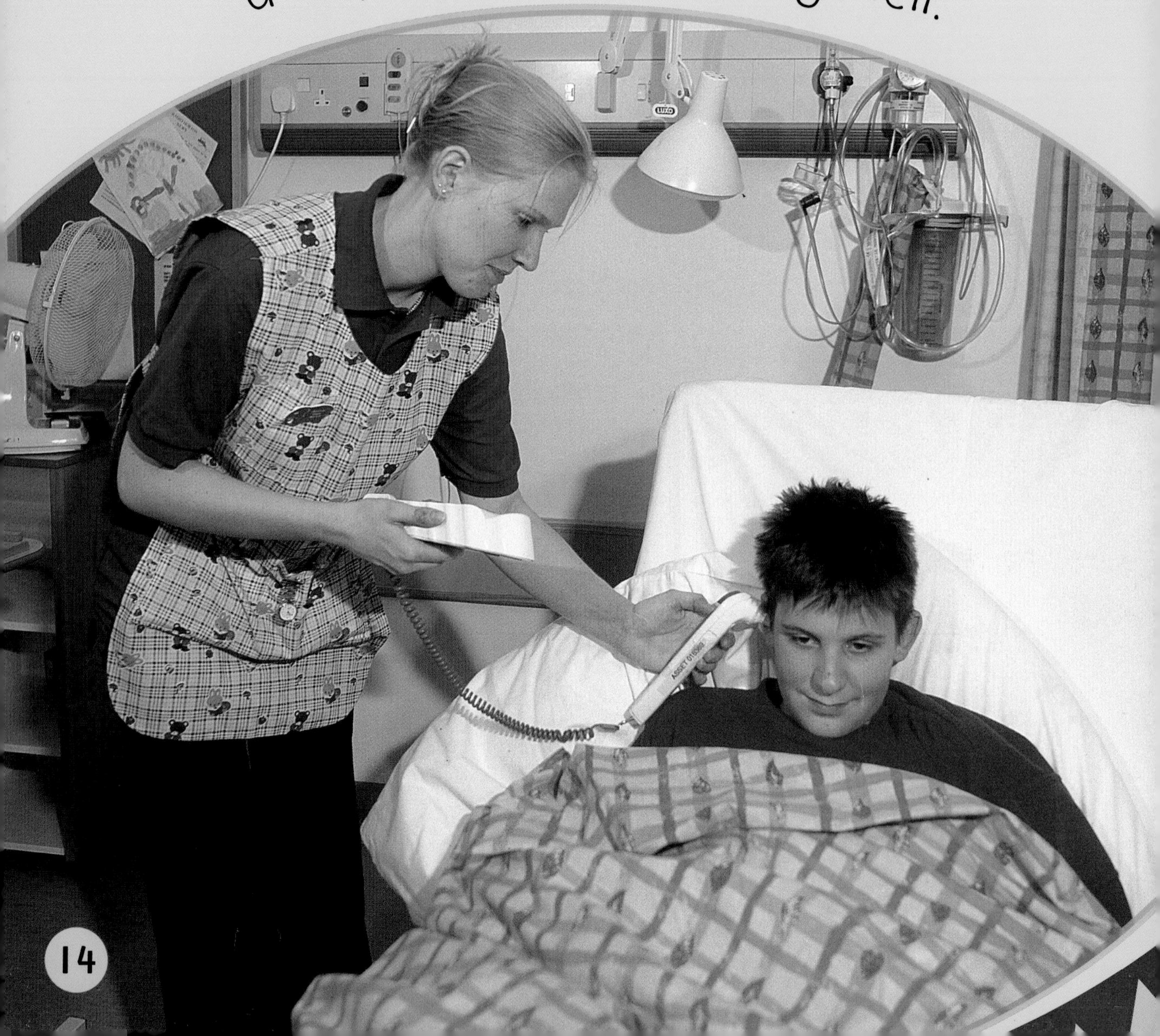

She talks to the parent
of a little boy who has
broken his leg.

Breaktime

16

It is very busy in the children's room.

An emergency

Anna talks to a new patient and listens to her chest.

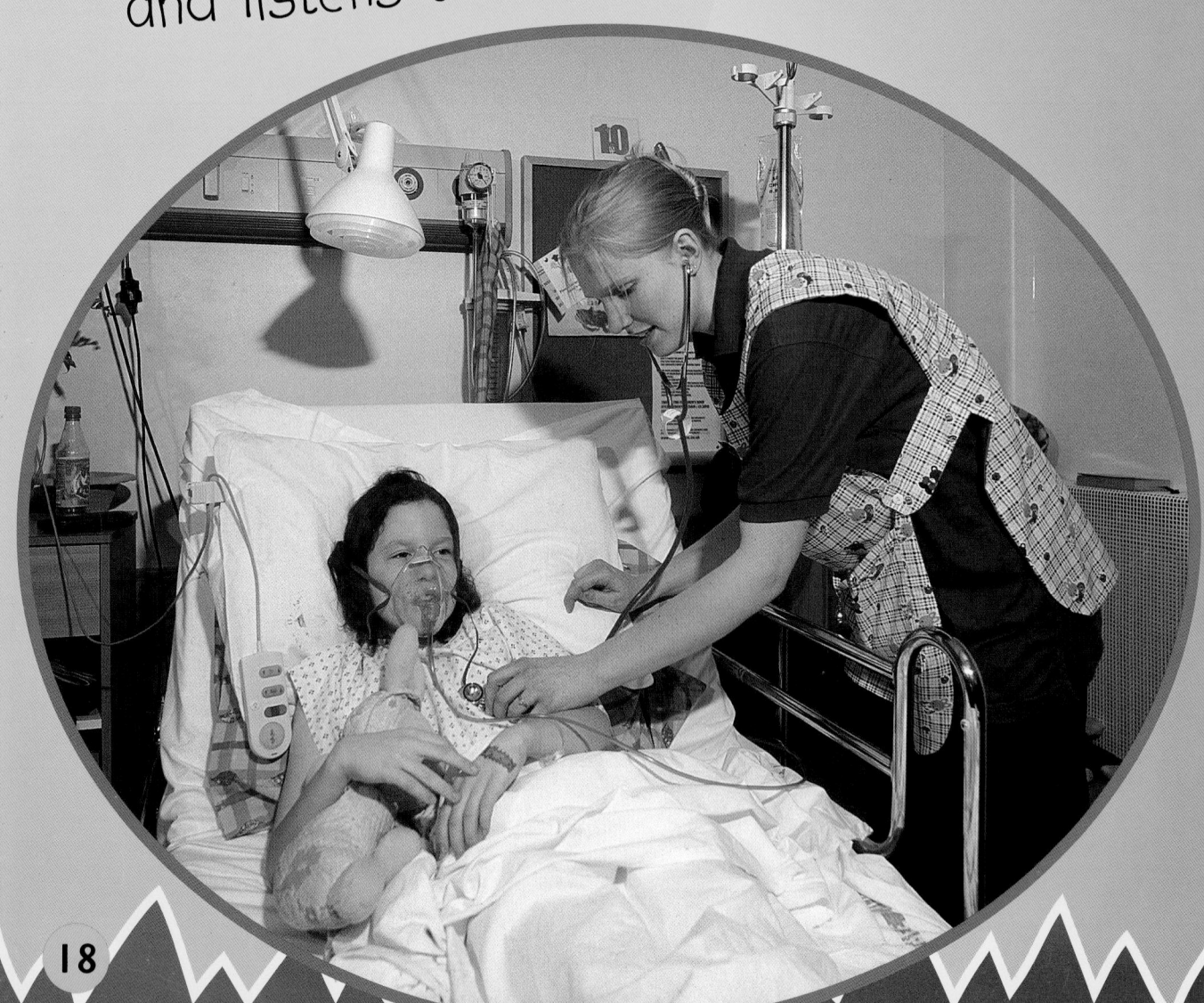

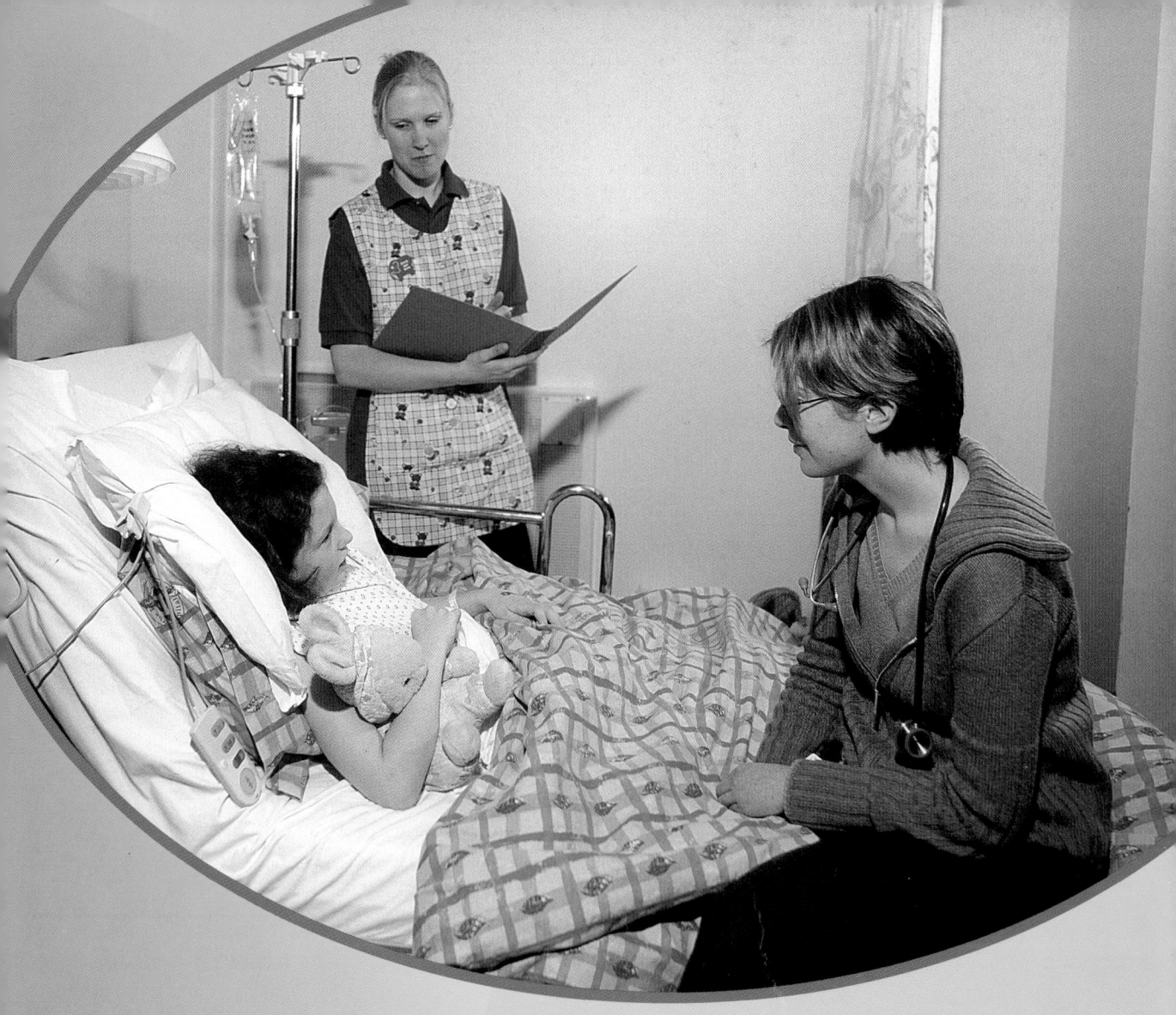

Doctor Tanya examines the patient and says she has to stay in hospital. Have you ever stayed in a hospital?

Looking after the patient

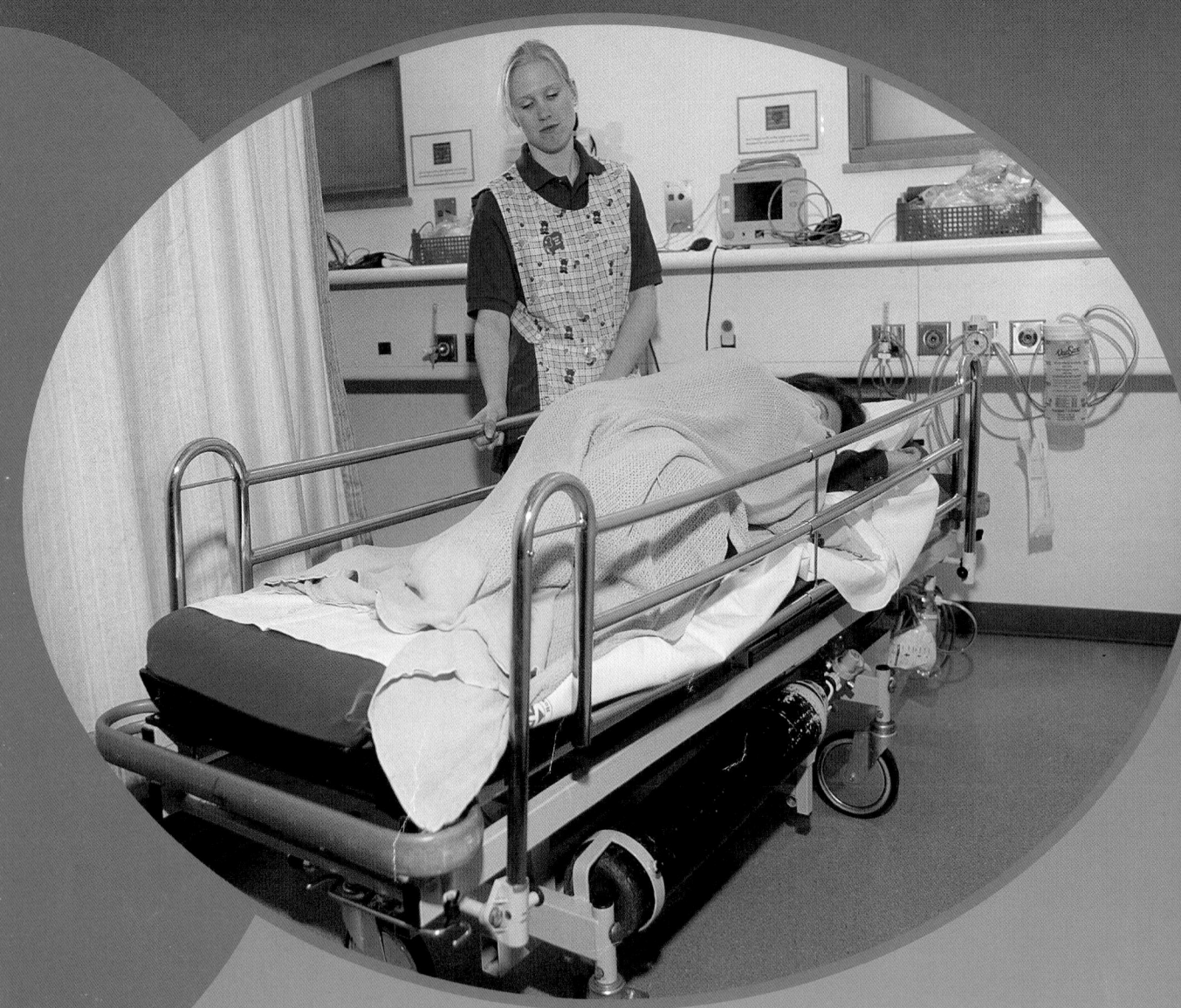

Anna goes with the patient
to the children's ward.

Main Entrance - All Wards & Departments

Finally it is time
for Anna to go home.

21

The day ends

Anna gets home from work and relaxes with her family.

22

zzzzzzzzz!

Then she goes to sleep.

Index

The end

Notes for adults

This series supports the young child's exploration of their learning environment and their knowledge and understanding of their world. The following Early Learning Goals are relevant to the series:
- Respond to significant experiences, showing a range of feelings when appropriate.
- Find out about events that they observe.
- Ask questions about why things happen and how things work.
- Find out about and identify the uses of everyday technology to support their learning.

The series shows the different jobs four professionals do and provides opportunities to compare and contrast them. The books show that like everyone else, including young children, they get up in the morning, go to bed at night, break for meals, and have families, pets and a life outside their work.

The books will help the child to extend their vocabulary, as they will hear new words. Some of the words that may be new to them in **A Day in the Life of a Nurse** are *hospital, patient, nightmare, X-ray, sling, temperature, examines* and *ward*. Since words are used in context in the book this should enable the young child to gradually incorporate them into their own vocabulary.

The following additional information may be of interest:
On the ward the nurse is responsible for the day-to-day care of patients and works in partnership with the doctor. She also offers support and advice to the patient's family. A broken limb may be made immobile by the use of a sling or traction.

Follow-up activities
The child could role play situations in a hospital ward. Areas could be set up to create a ward and a nurses' station. The child could also record what they have found out by drawing, painting or tape recording their experiences.